How a New Family Works

Rachel Gaillard Smook

Enslow Publishers, Inc.

40 Industrial Road   PO Box 38
Box 398   Aldershot
Berkeley Heights, NJ 07922   Hants GU12 6BP
USA   UK

http://www.enslow.com

Library of Congress Cataloging-in-Publication Data

Gaillard Smook, Rachel.
    Stepfamilies : how a new family works / Rachel Gaillard Smook.
        p. cm. — (Teen issues)
Includes bibliographical references and index.
ISBN 0-7660-1666-8 (hardcover : alk. paper)
  1. Stepfamilies—Juvenile literature. 2. Teenagers—Family
relationships—Juvenile literature. [1. Stepfamilies.] I. Title. II.
Series.
    HQ759.92 .G35   2001
    306.874—dc21

                                              00-012656

Printed in the United States of America

10 9 8 7 6 5 4 3 2

To Our Readers:
We have done our best to make sure all Internet addresses in this book were active and
appropriate when we went to press. However, the author and the publisher have no
control over and assume no liability for the material available on those Internet sites or
on other Web sites they may link to. Any comments or suggestions can be sent by e-mail
to comments@enslow.com or to the address on the back cover.

Illustration Credits: © Alternate Family magazine, p. 40; © Corel Corporation,
p. 48; Courtesy of Patty Debnam, p. 24; courtesy of the Gaillard/Frederick
family, p. 29; courtesy of the Martinez family, p. 17; courtesy of the
Phillips/Fuller family, p. 15; courtesy of Diane Smook, p. 9; courtesy of John F.
Souza photography, p. 35; Skjold Photos, pp. 52, 54.

Cover Photo: © Skjold Photos; Background © Corel Corporation.

Contents

Dedication

*This book is dedicated to Corbin,
child not of my body but of my heart
and to Clay,
my partner in parenting, love, friendship, and life*

Acknowledgments

I would like to make grateful acknowledgment to the following:

my parents, Rosemary Peduzzi and Frye Gaillard, for always putting parenting first and encouraging me without cease, and my stepmother, Nancy Gaillard, for her artful handling of her role;

the individuals and families with whom I have been privileged to work as a psychotherapist, for teaching me the many struggles, joys, and ways of living and healing that families create;

the children and families who shared their experiences with me for this book and who reminded me again that stepfamilies are normal families;

my colleagues and professors, for mentoring, teaching, and celebrating our craft;

and to Tracy, Kevin, Heather, Jodi, Kelli, Janice, and my wonderful community of family and friends, for being there every single time I have ever needed them.

1

What Is a
Stepfamily?

Zach, a sixth grader, got up early on the morning of his father's wedding. He dressed in a tuxedo and a top hat, and, a few hours later, walked down the aisle at his father's side with the wedding rings in his pocket. He watched with his father as the bride—his new stepmother—came down the aisle to join them. When it was time for his father and his stepmother to exchange rings, Zach stood at the altar, too, watching closely. Then the new couple presented a gift to Zach, and the person who married them explained that this ceremony did not just celebrate a marriage; it celebrated the formation of a family, of which Zach was an equal part.[1]

Families come in countless shapes and sizes. Often, families are thought of simply as including two married people and the children they have together. Although this kind of family is common, there are many variations. For example, some families have only one parent. Others have parents and also grandparents or cousins or aunts or uncles who all live together. Some parents are partners who have chosen not to marry. There are also millions of stepfamilies, just one of the many different kinds of families in the world today.

How Common Are Stepfamilies?

Many teens want their original parents to be together. If that is not possible, it sometimes feels uncomfortable. It can be hard to adjust when parents are not able to stay together, and even harder when a parent finds someone new to live with and to love. Young people often worry about their families being different from everyone else's. It may help to learn that being a member of a stepfamily is a very common experience. In fact, although the United States Census Department no longer keeps records of stepfamilies, experts think that soon there will be more stepfamilies than any other kind of family.[2]

Think about a typical class in an American school. If there were thirty students in that class, it is likely that ten of them would be members of stepfamilies right now. Fifteen of the students will become stepparents or stepchildren at some point in their lives.[3] That is half of all the kids in the class. Of the remaining half, some of the students would live with both of their original parents, others would live with only one parent, and the rest might be cared for by relatives or by guardians to whom they were not related. If one classroom can have that many different kinds of families in it, imagine how many there must be in the entire world.

Defining Stepfamilies

Even stepfamilies themselves can come in various shapes and sizes. Most of the time when people talk about stepfamilies, they mean those families that include a man, a woman, and his or her children, with one or both of the adults having been previously married. However, some researchers who study stepfamilies think that this definition leaves out a lot of people. For example, some experts think that it is important to include families in which the adults are not married to each other but live together with their children from previous marriages.[4] Research has shown that one out of every four stepfamilies falls into that category, and that two out of every three stepfamilies with married parents started out by living together first.[5]

It is important to know that some people feel that it is okay for adults to live together without being married and some people do not. Each family needs to decide for itself what it believes to be right. To understand stepfamilies, however, people need to use a broad definition to make sure that everyone is included. The Stepfamily Association of America, an organization that provides education and support to stepfamilies and professionals working with them, says that a stepfamily is made up of an adult couple, at least one of whom has a child from a previous relationship.[6]

Forming a Stepfamily

There are many ways in which stepfamilies are formed. All of these ways mean that the teen's original parents are no longer together. Sometimes this happens when parents divorce. At other times, the parents never lived together at all. Occasionally, a parent dies, and the stepfamily is formed when the parent who is still living finds another person to love.

Most people feel sad when their families go through these kinds of changes and losses. At times, it may be a relief when unhappy original parents decide to divorce. Regardless of the feelings about the divorce, joining a stepfamily can seem like a happy or an unhappy event. Sometimes it is a joy to have more people to love, and at other times it may seem more like a burden. Often,

Kinds of Stepfamilies

There are many ways in which teens can be a part of stepfamilies. Some of these include:

- Living with the original mother, her children, and a stepfather
- Living with the original father, his children, and a stepmother
- Living with an original parent, his or her children, and his or her lesbian or gay partner
- Being a part of a stepfamily in which both the parents have children from previous relationships
- Belonging to a stepfamily in which the new couple decides to have children together, in addition to the children from a prior relationship

In addition to these variations, some teens live full time with their stepfamilies, and some live with them part of the time or not at all.

Living with a stepfamily does not have to be bad—as portrayed in many fairy tales. This stepfamily is happily relaxing together on vacation.

teens feel some of each of these emotions, which can be confusing.

All of those feelings will be explored, as well as others that are common in stepfamilies. It is important to learn the ways stepfamilies are the same, by examining the challenges and opportunities that they all face. It is also important to remember that being a part of a stepfamily is a common and acceptable thing, even though at times it feels confusing. Millions and millions of kids are coping with learning to live in stepfamilies. Stepfamilies are normal families. Reading about others' experiences may help to make the challenges less daunting.

2

How a Stepfamily Is Formed

n many families, two adults meet first. They get to know one another, often fall in love, and sometimes marry. This couple does not have children when they first meet. In a stepfamily, one or both of the adults already have children when they begin to form their relationship. Becoming a family in this way is a very different experience from being born into one.

For teens to become part of a stepfamily, something has to happen to change the family into which they were born. Often this means that the original parents have chosen to divorce. Sometimes parents who were never married find new partners. Stepfamilies can also be formed when one of the biological parents dies and the remaining parent falls in love with someone new. These kinds of changes are often difficult and present very different challenges from those that affect families in which the adults form relationships before they have children.

Stepfamily Challenges

A stepfamily has a lot of challenges facing it. First, it has to go through all the practical parts of becoming a family, such as merging separate households, setting up new rules and expectations, and developing emotional connections. All the people in the family have to learn how to be a part of it, and each may have different ideas about what that means. Underlying all of that is the fact that the children involved may still be grieving the loss of their original families. Having a stepfamily form, even if it is a happy time, can bring up sad memories or confusing feelings about earlier family events.

It is important to know that feeling sad, angry, and confused when something happens to change a family is completely normal. Many people wish that their original parents could stay together and make each other happy. Even if the stepfamilies that follow mostly feel good, the teens in them may still miss the time when their first families were together.

Zach, a sixth grader, usually likes both of his stepfamilies. His parents are both married to new people, and his stepfather and stepmother both love him and get along with him well. Zach loves them, too, but this does not stop him from wondering why his biological parents could not continue to live together and love each other. "Sometimes I just wish my dad could live in my house," he said. "I don't understand why he has to be so far away." At times, Zach thinks it might be his fault that his mom and dad stopped having a relationship. He feels frustrated about having to move back and forth between two houses. Sometimes when he is with one family, he feels sad that he cannot be with the other. He also worries that his biological parents are still angry at each other.[1]

Zach's feelings are similar to the feelings of many kids in stepfamilies. He has a lot of questions about what happened to his original family, and some of those questions are hard to answer. For children, it is hard to imagine how people who love each other could stop feeling that way. Many assume that they somehow caused the problems between their parents, and they worry that their parents will stop loving *them* as well. It is important to remember that the separation of the original parents is *never* the fault of the children.

Parents are adults who are accountable for their own feelings and decisions. It may be very difficult when parents separate, but the responsibility for that belongs to the parents alone. Also, remember that the kind of love adults have for one another is different from the kind of love they feel for their children. Parents love one another in a romantic way first, then sometimes grow into loving each other as family members. Parents love their children as family from birth and sometimes from the time they know the mother is pregnant. Romantic love can end, but love for one's family is a different story. It is very sad when parents stop loving each other, but very rare for them to stop loving their kids. Parents who were attentive and loving to their children will still love them even if the family no longer lives together.

When a Parent Loses Contact

Occasionally, a parent may not be in contact with his or her child after a divorce. This is a terrible situation. Teens are very often deeply upset by it, and rightly so. There is no good explanation for why a parent would choose not to be in touch with his or her child. Teens who are abandoned in this way often feel very resentful and may also feel hatred toward the parent who left. At the same time, they may really love and miss that parent and wish for his or her return. Again, this situation is never the fault of the teen. A parent who stops being in contact with a child is entirely responsible for that decision. Teens living with this circumstance have every right to feel angry, confused, and sad. They may have those feelings even if the remaining parent is happily involved with someone new, just like teens in families in which both parents are a part of their lives.

Separation May Be a Relief

Kids may also feel happiness or relief that their parents are no longer together. Sam, an eighth grader, grew up seeing his parents fight all the time. "They were always yelling," he said. He sometimes worried about his mother's safety around his angry dad. When his parents decided to end their marriage, Sam was relieved. Although there have been some difficult adjustments in his new stepfamilies, he feels much better about his parents' new marriages than he did about the marriage they had to each other. "There's a lot less yelling in my life now," he said.[2]

It Takes Work to Build a Family

However people feel about the changes in the original family, forming a new family takes work. Relationships between adults are seldom always easy, even if they are very happy. Kids may be particularly afraid if a parent and stepparent argue. They may wonder if this means that another family breakup is likely. "My stepson worries that his father and I argue too much," said Mary, who has been married to her husband for two years, "but usually, what he considers arguments are just differences of opinion. We don't get angry very often, and we try to be careful not to argue in front of him. But if we don't agree at every turn, he gets afraid."[3] Mary's stepson is probably worried because he has already lived through the breakup of one family. He and others like him need to know that some disagreement (and even some argument) is normal between happy couples. No two people can agree on everything all the time. Managing these kinds of misunderstandings and others like them is part of the work that adults and teens in a new stepfamily need to learn to do.

Parents and stepparents also have work to do. Building a healthy relationship takes time and attention, exactly as in relationships between original parents. The difference is that in original families, the children were not there to see it happen. It is important to remember that parents and stepparents will have some bumps in the road as they learn to live with one another. Think about learning to ride a bicycle: Most people fall down a few times before they learn how to go where they want to go. Adults do the same thing when they form relationships. In stepfamilies, this is sometimes more complicated because adults also have to navigate the needs and feelings of their children. This does not mean that the children are in the way or that they should not be there; it is simply a fact of stepfamily life.

It is important to remember that it will take some time for a new family to agree on what it means to be a family. Imagine a class of ninth graders. If there are thirty people in the class, there are at least thirty families represented, probably more since many of those teens are likely to be

Living in a stepfamily can take a lot of work. People form an idea of what a "normal" family is like from their first family, and stepfamilies may not fit that mold. It can take a lot of work to resolve conflicts, but it is possible when people learn to talk about their feelings.

members of stepfamilies as well. It is unlikely that the rules in each of those thirty or more families are all the same. Houses will look different, people will behave differently, and there will be a variety of customs and experiences. Now imagine what it would be like if four or five of the people in that class tried to become a family themselves. Each student would bring different life stories to the new family, along with a wide range of expectations about what the family should look like and how it should work. It would take time and effort to learn how to bring all of those ideas together. This is exactly what happens when a stepfamily forms. Each member of the stepfamily will have his or her own ideas about what a "normal" family should be, and those ideas will not always be the same. This does not make one person right and another wrong. Learning to talk about and manage those differences and accepting that everyone needs to make an effort will help the family work better.

Teens Have Work to Do, Too

The ideas above are not suggestions that parents or teens in stepfamilies can do on their own. The whole family needs to work together to help, even if everyone does not feel like it. For teens who are resentful about their new stepfamilies, this can be quite a challenge, but parents on their own cannot make a family feel happy and work well. Teens can improve the quality of their own lives if they participate in building the new family. Their participation can also make

The American Academy of Child and Adolescent Psychiatry talks about stepfamily living. Some of its literature suggests things that stepfamilies need to do to become strong. These include:

- Accepting and mourning their losses
- Developing new skills in making decisions as a family
- Encouraging and strengthening new relationships between adults, between stepparents and stepchildren, and between stepsiblings
- Supporting one another
- Maintaining and supporting original parent-child relationships[4]

Stepfamilies, like other families, can include people from different races or cultural backgrounds.

it more likely that their needs are considered as the family creates its rules and expectations.

Adjusting to a new family structure is seldom easy. There are new rules to learn and new people to get to know. Sometimes it helps for parents and stepparents to spend some private time together learning about each other. Running errands together, going to a ballgame, decorating the house for a holiday, and similar activities can all provide opportunities for stepparents and stepchildren to learn about each other and to practice communicating well. Teens may sometimes need to be the ones to initiate such time together. Suggesting a fun activity, even something that takes only a few minutes, may help teens become more comfortable with their stepparents. Also, since the parents and stepparents are dealing with the challenge of forming their relationship under the watch of their children, it is important to allow them some time together. Stepparents who have never had children of their own are learning to be parents for the first time (which not even original parents manage perfectly), and teens can help by communicating openly, trying to be patient, and even occasionally cutting their stepparents some slack when they make mistakes.

3

Living in Two Houses

If biological parents do not live together, their children also often have more than one home. Sometimes the two homes are close together. Emily is a ninth grader whose father lives only a few streets away from her mother and stepfather. "It's great," she said. "I can walk from one house to the other anytime I want."[1]

Sam and Zach both have parents in different states, and visiting them takes much more effort. Zach sees his dad regularly, but Sam does not. Both find it difficult. Zach says that he would rather his dad lived nearby.[2] Sam, who has had some difficult times with his father, feels torn: On the one hand, the distance is okay with him because he is angry; on the other, Sam and his father are too far away to really have a chance to resolve their problems.[3]

The different houses in which teens in stepfamilies

spend their time may look nothing alike. The house that Zach shares with his mother and stepfather is filled with other children, including step- and half-siblings. In the house he shares with his father and stepmother, he is the only child. This means that time spent in each of his two homes is dramatically different. When Zach goes from one home to the other, he has to follow separate rules, adjust to different expectations by the adults, and communicate differently. At one house he is expected to clear his place at the table; at the other he is not. There are different rules for how much television is allowed. Even the way parents explain what they want is different in each family. This kind of adjusting can be hard work.

If teens have families in more than one home, they have the right to feel comfortable in both. This is why participating actively in developing strong relationships with stepfamily members is helpful for teens. Good relationships make it easier to feel at home in whichever house the person is spending time. (This does not mean it will be easy to move from one to the other and back again, just that the time spent in each is likely to be more comfortable.)

Each house contains an independent family, one or both of which will have stepfamily members as well as original family members. Jason, thirteen, an eighth grader with stepfamilies on both his mother's and his father's side, says that his two houses are "as different as night and day."[4] In his mother's house, he feels at ease, or, as he says, "more like myself." He feels like his father has "just completely changed personalities" since remarrying. Jason feels like he has had to get to know his father all over again (this time as a person in a happy relationship). He likes his stepmother, too, but finds the rules in their house to be very different from those to which he was accustomed. He has to try harder in his father's house than in his mother's house because there are stricter expectations and he just does not feel as relaxed. The two homes in which most stepchildren might live will have their own customs, rules, experiences, and expectations. Teens in stepfamilies often need to manage both sets of lifestyles in order to function well in two houses.

Who Makes the Rules?

In an original family, the rules are made by the parents. It can feel very threatening when a stepparent begins making rules, too. For one thing, there will often be some differences between the new rules and the old, and the old are more familiar. Although it is reasonable to expect stepparents to use sensitivity in communicating their expectations, it is important to remember that they have every right to have expectations. As adults sharing a home, both the parent and the stepparent have license to assert their needs about how it will function.

Leslie's mother remarried when Leslie was twelve years old and attending seventh grade. Leslie describes her

While many divorced parents are unable or unwilling to have family meetings, good communication can help a great deal to make living in two homes happier. Just as parents have the right to speak up about what they want their homes to be like, teens can do the same. It is important that teens speak as calmly and as clearly as possible about their needs and ideas. Adults will still make the decisions, but they can do that much more effectively if they know how the teens in their families really feel.

stepfamily experience as "completely nontraumatic." She says, "All three of my parents—my mom, my dad, and my stepdad—met together regularly to talk about me and to make sure they were all on the same page. It helped me not to feel in the middle."[5] Being clear that the adults agreed on their expectations of her also helped her to feel more at ease moving between two houses.

Stepsiblings

Sometimes, children must learn to deal with other children as well as stepparents. When a parent remarries or lives with someone new, that person often has children, too. When children of different parents live together in stepfamilies they are called stepsiblings or stepbrothers and stepsisters. Hannah was fourteen when her father moved in with her stepmother and her stepmother's son. "A lot of people talked about my 'instant brother,'" she said, "but to me he felt like a friend from school. I love him a lot, but he never felt like my actual brother."[6] In reality, Hannah's stepbrother is *not* her "actual brother." They do not share the same original parents. It is natural for them to feel more like schoolmates or friends. Maybe they will come to view each other more as siblings, or maybe not. Either outcome is acceptable, particularly since they have learned how to live well together and share equally in their family.

Stepsiblings may also find themselves in the unfortunate position of not getting along. Teens may feel that they dislike a new stepsibling, when what they really dislike is having to be in a stepfamily at all. Teens may also feel jealous of a stepsibling, especially if that person is getting more attention or having an easier time adjusting to the new family. It is important to remember that the formation of a stepfamily and the changes that creating a new family entails are not the fault of other kids. Teens and families in a tense situation need to work together to find a way of maintaining civility at home, even if the stepsiblings never become friends.

It is unlikely that Hannah's dad and her new stepmother have equal feelings about both children. It is probably unrealistic to expect that a stepparent will feel the same way toward a stepchild as the original parent does. (After all, the stepchild probably does not love the parent and stepparent in the same way, either.) Often, stepchildren complain that their stepparents "favor" their own children above the stepchildren. Like Cinderella, most stories about stepparents teach that they are "wicked." It is not wicked for a stepparent to have special love for his or her own child. However, it is important for the family to work together to be sure that all the kids are being treated fairly, even if the relationships are different from person to person. If this does not happen, it is a setup for family problems.

Half-siblings

Original parents and stepparents may also have children together. Sam has two half sisters whom his mother and stepfather had together. For Sam, this has been a happy experience. He says, "If not for my stepdad, I wouldn't have my little sisters, and I can't imagine not having my little sisters."[7] Zach loves his half-siblings from his mother and stepfather, too, but worries what his life will feel like if his father and stepmother, who do not currently have children, decide to add a baby to the family. He likes having a place to go in which to get a lot of one-on-one attention from adults. He feels concerned about losing his place.[8]

Zach's and Sam's parents will need to work hard to

It can be both a challenge and a joy for teenagers when a parent and stepparent decide to have a baby together.

assure that Zach and Sam know that their places in their families cannot be filled by other children. They can do this in part by making sure that there is special time for just the boys and their parents. For example, it is reasonable for Zach to expect that if his father and stepmother have a baby, he will have time alone with them while the baby naps or after he or she goes to bed. He can also request some activities just with his dad, time that the two of them can get away without a baby in tow. Sam and his mother sometimes leave the girls with his stepfather and spend an afternoon alone.

4

Stepparents as Parents

M any teens have two parents. Today, it is not at all uncommon to have more than that. A lot of teens have at least one stepparent, and a large number have two. A child whose mother or father dies and whose remaining parent remarries will have two parents, but not the original two. What is it like when someone new joins a family and becomes a parent?

This question may be answered by thinking about what it is like when someone becomes the parent of a new baby rather than an older stepchild. By the time a baby is born, parents have spent a long time planning, thinking ahead, and getting excited.

Often parents fall in love with the child they imagine long before the actual birth. Even after the baby is born, though, it takes time for them to learn about who she is, what her likes and dislikes are, how she behaves, and what she needs from her parents. Parents take a long time getting to know their infants and learning about how to care for them well.

In stepfamilies, the children are already there when the stepparent first comes into the picture. One of the ways that stepfamilies are different from original families is that new husbands and wives become instant parents to their partner's children, writes Bobbie Reed in *Merging Families: A Step-by-Step Guide for Blended Families*. However, she notes, "the instant parent is not presented with a tiny infant, which is a precious reminder of moments of shared love. Instead, the child represents the spouse's previous intimate relationship with someone else. And the child comes ready-made, complete with ideas, values, opinions, preferences, and living habits. Seldom are these totally compatible with the expectations of the new stepparent."[1]

Stepparents, like birth parents, need time to get to know their new children. Joining a stepfamily can be like jumping onto a bus when the bus is already moving. Stepchildren may have difficulty with the sudden addition of someone who is in a parent position but who has not yet had the time to really learn about his or her new children. It may be hard for teens to change well-established ways of living, and the stepparent may seem like an intruder. Seventh-grader Ted says, "My mom never made us do anything we didn't want to do. And now that my stepdad is there, we have all kinds of chores we didn't have before. What was wrong with the way my mom did things?"[2]

The answer to that is: maybe nothing. However, what worked for a family that only included one parent does not work in Ted's new family, which has two parents and several other children. Ted was angry at his stepfather for changing things, but the stepfather was only doing what he needed to do to help the stepfamily function. It is essential for Ted and others who feel as he does to remember that being angry about a change is normal, but blaming someone for causing it is seldom helpful.

Taking Time

It is also important to remember that everything is unlikely to work perfectly from the beginning. Birth parents know their children well, including knowing how far they can be pushed. (Again, it took them a long time to learn all of this.) Hannah did not mind people coming into her room unannounced, but did not want her belongings to be moved.[3] Zach usually liked new foods once he tried them, but needed patience from his parents if he felt hesitant about taking the first bite.[4] Zach's and Hannah's parents already knew these things about them and could be careful not to cross the line.

Their stepparents had to learn over time, and, until then, sometimes did things that Zach and Hannah found upsetting. It would have been easy for Hannah and Zach to assume that this meant that their stepparents were unloving, mean, or untrustworthy, but in each case the problem was really just that the stepparents were new at their stepparenting jobs. Think again about the bicycle: It takes time to learn to ride smoothly.

The same is true for teens who are getting to know their new stepparents. "I knew what drove my mom crazy," Hannah says. "My stepmom was a total mystery at first. I was afraid I would do something to make her mad without even meaning to."[5] It is important to remember that everyone in a new stepfamily—parents and children alike—is struggling a bit with getting to know new people and adjusting to new roles. Some problems are bound to occur. Talking about the problems calmly and without blame can smooth the way to resolving them. Teens as well as parents can take some responsibility for this. It is hard for people to listen when they are angry. If there has been an argument, it may help to wait until tempers cool before starting a discussion about how things are going in the family. It may also help for teens to take some time out to calm down before trying to talk through a frustrating event.

Loyalty and Love

Stepchildren often experience conflict about loyalty. They may wonder if it is unfair to have good feelings about a stepparent, and if doing so means they really are not

Teens in stepfamilies often like having more parents and siblings in their lives. Stepfamilies provide the opportunity to have extra people to help celebrate the important events in a teen's life.

faithful to their original parents. Hannah worried about how her mom would feel if she participated in her dad's wedding. "I worried that she would feel displaced," she said. "I worried that she would think I wouldn't love her as much now that there was another mother figure in the family."[6]

In *Stepkids: A Survival Guide for Teenagers in Stepfamilies*, Ann Getzoff and Carolyn McClenahan talk about love in families of all types. They write, "Sometimes stepkids really want to like or even love their stepparent, but they are afraid of being disloyal to their real mom or dad if they let themselves get close. It is important to know that you have lots of love available for all the important people in your life, and you are not betraying your real mom or dad if you love your stepmom or stepdad. You have the right to love them both if you want to." [7]

But since it takes a long time for stepparents and their stepchildren to really get to know each other, expecting instant love is probably unrealistic. Getzoff and McClenahan write, "If you like each other, that's wonderful. If you don't like each other, that's okay, too, because you can still learn to live in the same house with some degree of mutual respect."[8]

It is okay for teens to love, or not to love, their stepparents. Stepparents may or may not love their stepchildren. Being in a stepfamily can be good either way. Think of all the people with whom teenagers can have healthy, comfortable interactions without feeling love: teachers, doctors, neighbors, parents' friends, and so on. The trick is to maintain respect in the relationship.

5

Parents as Partners

In most original families, the parents fall in love and learn how to be in a relationship with one another before having children. In stepfamilies, teens not only need to mourn the loss of the relationship between their parents, but also they witness a parent in the early stages of a new romantic relationship. That, says Sam, "is *weird*."[1]

Certainly it is something that many kids never see. Jason says, "I never knew my dad before he was with my mom. I was surprised how he turned out to be when my mom wasn't there. I had to get to know my dad all over again."[2] When Jason's dad fell in love and remarried, Jason saw yet another side of his father that he had not imagined was there. Leslie had a similar experience. She says, "My mom had three boyfriends at one time!" She thought her friends could reasonably be expected to try out multiple boyfriends, but felt that was odd behavior for a mother.[3] It was uncomfortable for her to imagine her parent as a sexual being.

Feelings About Seeing Adults in Love

Hannah, Leslie, Jason, and Sam all report feeling very happy that their parents have someone to love. "I was worried about my mom when she was alone," Sam says. "Now I know she's not lonely."[4] To them, this is worth the "weirdness" of seeing them act and speak like new lovers. Zach is not sure about this. He loves his stepparents and wants his biological parents to be happy, but he is very sorry that his biological parents cannot be happy together. He sometimes feels uncomfortable seeing the affection expressed around his two homes and wishes that his parents could have those feelings for one another instead of for two outsiders.[5]

These are all normal feelings. As Sam notes, when biological parents are deeply unhappy together, when they fight often, or when being in the original family feels scary, having a stepfamily may even be a relief. He remembers that when his parents were together, "Everyone was so miserable the kids got no attention at all." He feels as though his mom is more available to him now that she is not spending all her energy on an unhappy relationship. "I'm glad my mom found my stepdad because he's nice to her and he takes care of her," he says.[6]

Many kids are also angry that their original families did not try harder to work things out so they could stay together. Occasionally parents break up without really working on their relationship, but more often they have tried everything they can think of to save it. They divorce because they realize that being apart will be much healthier in the long run than staying together and feeling miserable.

Coping With Arguments

The fact that the original family did not remain together often makes arguments between parent and stepparent seem a great deal more frightening. Teens may fear another loss, another separation, another time of turmoil for their families. It is natural to feel afraid when parents and stepparents fight. It may help for a scared stepchild to ask questions about the relationship after the fight is over. It may also help if teens remind their parents that it feels scary to see and hear them arguing.

It is *not* helpful to scream, threaten parents, or say that another parent would handle problems better. This last remark can be very tempting for teens who are resentful of their stepparents or who blame the stepparents for the breakup of the original family. But blaming or rejecting a stepparent does not make things better for anyone, teens and other adults included. It is important to remember that the breakup of the original family had nothing to do with the stepparent. The parents in the original family

Here are some comments teens can make to help their families understand that fighting is upsetting and that they need help understanding what is happening:

- "I feel scared when you fight."
- "I'm afraid you are going to break up."
- "It would help me if you would speak more quietly."
- "I don't understand why you are arguing."
- "I wish you weren't so angry at each other."

were having trouble before the stepparent came into the picture. Even if the stepparent and parent became romantically involved with each other before the family officially split up, they did so because the original family was already in trouble.

It is also important to remember that the adults, not the children, are the ones responsible for resolving their arguments. It is okay for a teen to speak up about the way the argument affects him or her, but after that the adults in the family have to decide what they are going to do. Teens cannot fix things that are going poorly between their parents any more than they can cause a relationship to break down in the first place.

It may help to remember that parents learn a lot about themselves and about relationships when they go through a divorce. They may now know more than they did in the original family about what a family needs to stay together. Parents do not want to have another family loss any more than their children do.

Even people who get along well sometimes fight. Family therapist John Gottman, an expert on marital relationships, has learned that for every five positive interactions a couple has, there is likely to be one that is negative.[7] This means that some disagreement is normal and even predictable. It can be scary to see, but it does not necessarily mean that the family will not survive.

Worrying About the Other Parent

When only one of the parents in the original family is involved in a new relationship, teens may worry about the feelings of the parent who remains alone. Hannah was worried about her mother being lonely now that her father was in a new relationship. She says, "It sort of magnified to

Being part of a stepfamily often means that teenagers have large extended families.

me how alone she was. I thought it would be terrible for her to know my dad was in love with someone else or to see them together. I wanted to protect her from that."[8]

Hannah's mother may well have had feelings of loneliness, and may have found it quite difficult to see her former husband with his new wife. This is sad, but normal. There is nothing Hannah could have done that would have protected her mother from these feelings.

The Adult Relationship Is Important

Parents and stepparents need to pay special attention to their relationships. The challenges that stepfamilies face put extra pressure on the relationships between adults.

This means that the adults in the family will need time together to concentrate on keeping their relationship happy. Researchers report that the stability of a stepfamily depends on how satisfied the parent and stepparent are with their relationship. If the parent and stepparent have a happy relationship, the stepfamily is better able to face all its challenges, while parents in an unhealthy relationship cannot cope with the extra demands that stepfamily living places on them.[9] Some research indicates that stepchildren and their stepparents get along much better if the parent and stepparent are happy.[10] So, even though it may be awkward to observe parents and stepparents hugging, kissing, talking in silly voices, or otherwise showing affection to one another, it is important that they feel good about each other. Affection is good for everyone.

6

Gay Stepfamilies

here are many ways for families to look, to act, and to form. Any one family is likely to be quite different from the family next door. That includes stepfamilies. People in the same family do not always have the same skin color, or believe the same things, or have the same religious values. Jason identifies this as one of the benefits of having several families at once: "You get exposed to quite a variety of values, new values, and also new interests, new thoughts, and incredibly different kinds of people." He adds, "Different isn't necessarily wrong!"[1]

One way that families may differ is in the kinds of partnerships that are made between adults. Say the word "family," and most people will probably picture a group involving a man, a woman, and their children. This is not the only kind of family in the world. Many families have two women heading them, or two men. In these families, the parents are usually homosexual. Other words for homosexual include "lesbian" for women and "gay" for men and women. These families are no less "real" than families in which one partner is male and the other female, but they may face particular social pressures. It is important for people to learn about and understand gay families and gay stepfamilies in order to reduce the effects of that pressure on the family's children.

A Gay Stepfamily Does Not Mean a Different Stepfamily

Jason's mom and dad were married before he was born, and they later divorced. His dad then fell in love with a new woman, whom he later married and who became Jason's stepmother. Jason's mom also formed a new partnership, and hers was with a woman as well. This woman is now Jason's stepmother also. When Jason describes his two families, he talks about many of the same issues that children in heterosexual (also called straight) stepfamilies experience. He says, "Gay stepfamilies are not different! You make all the same changes and adjustments as with straight stepfamilies. I should know; I've got both." Jason thought that finding out that his parents were divorcing was much more difficult than finding out that his mother was gay or than adjusting to a lesbian stepmother.[2]

A number of children in gay stepfamilies would not agree to be interviewed for this book because they were concerned about the possibility of presenting an image that gay stepfamilies are different from other kinds of stepfamilies. None of these teens believed his or her gay stepfamilies were much different from their straight ones.

In gay stepfamilies, most of the adjustments teens have to make are the same as in any other kind of stepfamily. There are new customs and expectations to learn, new people to get to know, changes in household routines, and grieving for the loss of the original family. As with other stepfamilies, there are also a lot of joys.

Prejudice

Most of the problems experienced in gay stepfamilies seem to be the result of other people's prejudices and misinformation. In *Lesbian Stepfamilies: An Ethnography of Love,* Janet Wright interviewed a number of people and found that their concerns were similar to those of people in straight stepfamilies. Many of the people Wright interviewed talked about being and feeling normal, although they suffered the effects of other people's prejudices against them.[3]

Prejudice happens when someone makes a judgment (usually negative) about another person without sufficient evidence. Sometimes, prejudice is racial or ethnic in nature. People who are biased think that those they look down on have bad qualities such as being less smart, capable, safe, or trustworthy because of their different skin colors or accents. But people are also prejudiced about religious beliefs, sexuality, and any number of other everyday differences that normal people have from one another. Of course, someone's skin color has nothing to do with how smart or friendly or capable or safe or trustworthy that person is. Likewise, the sexual orientation of the parents in a stepfamily has nothing to do with how well that family functions. Learning about people who are different from one another helps reduce the danger of prejudice.

Jason finds that educating his friends about his gay

A national parenting magazine for gay, lesbian, bisexual, transgender parents & their children

ALTERNATIVE FAMILY
m a g a z i n e

JAN/FEB 2000
Volume 3, No. 1

$4.95 USA
$6.95 CD

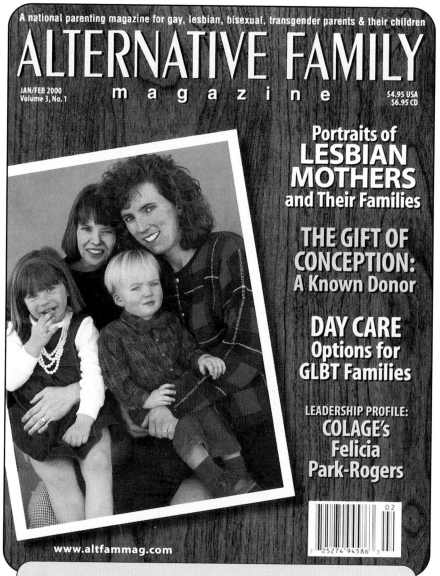

Portraits of
LESBIAN MOTHERS
and Their Families

THE GIFT OF CONCEPTION:
A Known Donor

DAY CARE
Options for GLBT Families

LEADERSHIP PROFILE:
COLAGE's Felicia Park-Rogers

www.altfammag.com

02
7 25274 94586 3

The challenges of living in a stepfamily in which the parents are gay are the same as those in a family with heterosexual parents, say teens in gay families.

stepfamily has helped. His school is also gay-friendly, which means that his teachers and most of the other students are not prejudiced against people who are homosexual. The openness and respect of his relationships with his stepmom, mom, and friends have strengthened his stepfamily experience, as has talking about his questions and concerns. All of this has taught Jason that a gay family and a straight one are not that different after all.

7

How Does It Feel to Be in a Stepfamily?

The message of the Cinderella story is that being a part of a stepfamily is always terrible. Teens may feel afraid to join one because stepfamilies are so often shown as bad, but the experience is not usually all horrible. As in any kind of family, there are likely to be both terrible as well as wonderful moments and everything in between. Stepfamilies change and grow with time, as do other kinds of families, and teens themselves. Yet some feelings are very common to people in stepfamilies.

Sadness and Grief

Teens have to go through some kind of change or loss to even become a part of a stepfamily in the first place, and it is inevitable that there will be some sad feelings associated with that. They may miss parents they no longer see or no longer see as often. They will also miss the idea of the family they used to have, and will probably feel sad that they do not have it anymore, even if their new stepfamilies are happy or their original families were troubled.

Sadness is also inevitable if a parent has died. The new family may be very happy, but the death of a parent will still be a tremendous loss. It is okay to never stop missing a parent who has died, even if the pain becomes less acute over time. Seeing the other parent move on and find happiness may partly be a relief, but it may also partly reinforce how sad it is that the death occurred.

Sadness about an original family may be especially painful if the new stepfamily is having trouble. It may feel like there is no such thing as a happy family, and people may long for a time in their lives that felt better. This can be especially difficult for teenagers, for whom life often feels rocky enough without the added strain of families breaking up and reforming. The sadness often lifts in time as the family settles. If a teen is feeling sad most of the time, it is important that he or she ask for help.

Anger and Frustration

Stepchildren may also feel a lot of anger or frustration, and much of this often has to do with adapting to change. It takes patience to learn to live in new ways, alter one's behavior, and deal with new family members. Ted feels angry about all the new chores he and his brother have now that they are part of a stepfamily. He feels that it would have been easier for him if his mother had just stayed single.[1]

Change is seldom easy. What often makes it harder for teens in stepfamilies is that they usually have no choice in the matter. If a teen decides to go to a new summer camp, for example, he or she will have some difficulty in learning the new routines and making new friends, but the change will be easier because going to the new camp was something the teen really wanted to do. This is not often the case when an original family breaks up, and it can be frustrating to have no control over those kinds of decisions.

Parents sometimes make the choice to separate even when their children desperately wish that they would remain together. Stepfamilies also form in this way, because it is the choice of the adults to move in together or marry. Jason, who is now fourteen, remembers that his dad's new girlfriend moved in with the family rather quickly. No one really talked to him about what was happening. He says, "More time to get to know her would have been helpful, but mainly I think talking more would have made it better."[2] The adjustment was particularly difficult for Jason, who was not able to participate in this life-altering decision.

Teens are also often angry at their original parents. Emily feels that her parents must not have tried very hard to work on their marriage. She was angry at her father when he moved out, and later became upset with her mother for not being the kind of person to whom her father wanted to be married.[3] But parents usually take their relationships very seriously and are sad and angry themselves when the relationships end. Most of the time, they have tried as hard as they can.

It is also normal to feel angry when a parent dies. A lot of times when people are angry at someone who has died, they then feel guilty about it. It may help to know that anger is a normal part of grief. Almost everybody who loses someone important to them feels anger. Teens with living but divorced parents sometimes feel angry at them; feeling that way about a parent who is no longer alive is predictable and okay. A death is very disruptive and causes changes that nobody wanted. Anger in that situation will probably pass in time.

Feelings of anger toward stepparents are also normal. Stepparents may be blamed for all the changes that are taking place in the family. Also, because stepparents and stepchildren may hurt each other's feelings accidentally when they are in the process of getting to know each other, it can be easy for teens to view their stepparents as enemies.

While it is normal to be angry and to resent the changes that have happened in the family, staying angry for a long time is likely to make things more and more difficult. Arguments will start faster and will be harder to resolve. If a teen is feeling angry most of the time, it is important to talk about it and possibly to get some help in managing it.

Confusion

People in stepfamilies may also feel confused. Often this has to do with not knowing the new routines very well yet. It can feel similar to being in a new school on the first day, not knowing where the cafeteria is or who the teachers are or what room classes are in. These things can all be learned with time and patience; so can the routines and expectations of a stepfamily.

When original families break up, confusion often results. Most teens do not know exactly why breakups occur. Even if they have seen parents being very unhappy together for a long time, they may not know why the difficulty began in the first place. It can be helpful to ask. Sometimes parents need to know that kids are feeling confused so that they can help resolve any unanswered questions.

Joy and Love

Often there is great joy when a parent falls in love. Hannah and Leslie were both fourteen when this happened in their own families. Hannah felt sorry that her parents did not have people to love and recognized how much happier her father felt once he met his new wife.[4] Feeling happy about new family members is just as common and acceptable as feeling sad. Leslie says, "I thought stepfamilies were miserable as a rule. I thought I might be doing something wrong because I liked mine so much."[5]

There is nothing wrong with liking a stepfamily or with being happy or comfortable as a member of one. Zach highlights one of the biggest perks of having stepparents: "I have four sets of grandparents!" He also feels that having more family members means that there are more people to love him.[6] If members of stepfamilies can talk about their experiences and can work together to resolve problems that arise, there is no reason why being part of a stepfamily cannot be very joyful. A stepfamily will never replace an original family, but that is not its job. If everyone can remember that, they can get to work on making it the most satisfying new family it can be.

It is also okay to feel love for new members of the family. Feeling love is as normal as not feeling it. The love does not have to be exactly the same as love for one's original parent, either. It can be more like love for a friend, a teacher, or another important person in a teen's life. Whatever kind of love develops in the family, love itself is a normal emotion.

Feelings About Stepsiblings and Half-siblings

All of these feelings—love, joy, confusion, anger, sadness—have largely been discussed as connected to stepparents. These same sets of feelings are also predictable in relation to stepsiblings and half-siblings. When a stepparent's children join the family or when a new baby is born, the experience may be very difficult or very happy. Most likely, there will be elements of each.

Sometimes, just living with other children can be hard to handle. Teens may suddenly find themselves sharing bedrooms or bathrooms, feeling jealous about how other kids in the family are treated, or watching friendships develop between some stepsiblings but not others. It can be hard for teens to carry around uncomfortable feelings alone. It is important for teens in stepfamilies to talk about their circumstances. Getting support from friends can be especially meaningful.

It is also important that teens talk about how they feel with their families. Working out a way to share bedrooms or bathrooms so that everyone feels comfortable can go a long way toward preventing arguments and eliminating conflicts. It can help to say something like, "I'm tired of always fighting about how long everybody takes getting ready in the bathroom in the morning. Let's just decide ahead of time how much time is fair so that we will not have to argue about it anymore." It is important to know that guessing at how someone feels or what he or she thinks is not nearly as easy as asking the person directly. If family members get used to talking to each other about their feelings and needs, a lot of misunderstandings can be avoided.

One of the hardest things for teens in stepfamilies to deal with is simply not liking a stepsibling. Sometimes that happens because the people involved are just very different people who might never have gotten along under any circumstances. In that case, it is probably best to come up with a set of shared expectations about how to lessen the stress of having to live together.

Often, though, feelings of anger and hostility are really not about the stepsibling. If a teen is angry about being in

Sometimes, teens in stepfamilies develop crushes on each other. Though it is normal for teens to have romantic feelings, stepfamily life is considerably easier if teens living in the same house do not become romantically involved.

a stepfamily, he or she may direct that anger toward one person in it. It may be easier to feel hatred toward a stepsibling than to feel it toward the more vague problems of having family life change, watching parents fall in love, or feeling hurt about the loss of the original family. It is important that teens who are having trouble coping get some help in sorting out those feelings.

Another tricky situation may arise if stepsiblings form crushes on each other. It is normal for teens to have sexual or romantic feelings and want to explore them. Being attracted to someone a teen lives with can be both exciting and scary. But such attractions can have big consequences, so it is important to think very carefully before getting involved with a stepsibling. What if the attraction fades? What would it be like to share a house with an ex-boyfriend or ex-girlfriend?

Parents would probably feel uncomfortable about this kind of relationship, so teens might have to hide it from them. What would it be like to have to lie all the time? What if the teens were caught? What if there was an argument or a breakup? How would it be possible to hide that?

The problem with attraction between stepsiblings is not so much about the feelings themselves as what happens when the feelings are acted on. Most teen relationships do not last forever. Living in a stepfamily will be a lot easier if teens find boyfriends and girlfriends outside the home.

In any case, these feelings can be managed. The same things that help in dealing with feelings about stepparents—talking over feelings, giving oneself time to adjust—will probably help in dealing with emotions about other kids in the family.

8

Resources, Ways to Help, and Warning Signs

There are a lot of ways to work through and deal with the experience of being part of a stepfamily. Before discussing resources, it is important to be able to recognize some of the warning signs that show something is wrong and really needs attention in the family.

Warning Signs

Warning signs that teens are having a particularly hard time may include grades that suddenly drop or that are worse overall than what is normal for them. People may have trouble sleeping or may want to sleep all the time. (Of course, teenagers need a lot of sleep; too much sleep represents a problem only if it exceeds what is usual for most teens.) Any sudden change in weight may signal that coping with the stepfamily has become overwhelming. Getting sick often or having unusual headaches and stomachaches is another sign that there is too much stress. If teens fight, steal, or run away, this is very serious and needs attention immediately. Withdrawing from friends or activities that used to be fun is another warning sign.

Sometimes teens turn to alcohol or drugs to help them manage feelings of discomfort, pain, or unhappiness. Using alcohol or drugs numbs the feelings but does not make them go away. Although the numbness can be a temporary relief, a teen will still have to deal with unpleasant feelings and a possible addiction when the drugs have worn off. Addiction can cause all sorts of difficulties, including trouble concentrating, academic failure, loss of friendships and other relationships, financial crises, illness, and even death. These possibilities are too damaging to make it worth it to even try drugs or alcohol. If a teen begins using alcohol or drugs, help is needed right away. If a parent is abusing alcohol or drugs, the parent needs help, too. Even if the parent will not get help, support is available for kids with parents who are addicts.

Any time unpleasant feelings outnumber pleasant ones, it may be time to seek help. No one likes feeling sad or angry all the time, and having those feelings constantly in the house can make it hard for the stepfamily to move forward and develop good relationships. Some degree of these feelings is normal, but if these feelings seem to be affecting the teen's or the family's routines for a long time, it is important to get some help to work through them.

Sometimes when people feel bad more than they feel good, they begin to believe that life is simply not worth living. Other times, they believe that ending their lives would either punish the people around them or make things easier for them. It is never safe to keep these feelings private.

Sometimes, teens in stepfamilies turn to alcohol and drugs to numb their feelings of unhappiness. Though the initial feeling can be relief, alcohol and drugs only make the problems worse in the end.

If someone begins to feel that life is hopeless or that killing himself or herself is the only answer, that person needs to get help immediately. A teen who recognizes these feelings in a friend must tell an adult right away. If an adult is asked for help but does not provide it, it is crucial to ask someone else, and to keep asking until someone responds. It is a life-and-death situation.

Another thing that needs immediate attention is physical or sexual abuse. Anyone who is being touched in a way that feels bad or uncomfortable, whether by a member of the family or by someone else, needs to tell a trusted adult quickly. Often, teens in this situation feel ashamed or guilty, and this sometimes prevents them from asking for help. A child who is being abused by a stepparent may worry that telling someone about it would mean that his or her biological parent has to go through another family breakup or loss. It is important to remember that it is never okay for an adult or older teen to touch a smaller child sexually or to cause a child physical injury. Not telling is much more dangerous than telling, even if it feels uncomfortable.

Getting Help

If any of these warning signs is present, help is available from psychologists and social workers who are trained to work with teens and families. They know a lot about how to help when families feel unhappy. They also know who to call if a teen is unsafe for any reason, such as being abused or feeling suicidal.

People sometimes worry that seeing a therapist means they are crazy or sick. However, many people who are not the least bit crazy or sick seek mental health services. It is important to attend to mental health, just as it is important to attend to physical health. If some part of a person's body

Depression and suicidal feelings sometimes arise when problems of living in stepfamilies are not discussed. If those feelings arise, get help immediately.

were bothering him (for example, a sore throat that would not go away), that person would probably call a doctor for assistance. When people have unhappy feelings that will not go away, they can call a psychologist, a social worker, or another therapist. Think about the medical doctor: When the illness is better, the person no longer needs to see the doctor. The same is true of visiting a psychologist or a social worker. When the person feels better, the therapist's job is done. As with medical doctors, people can always return later if something needs more attention.

Being in therapy is likely to bring a mix of very good feelings and also difficult experiences. It can be exhausting to have to face unpleasant emotions, experiences, or behaviors. However, facing these feelings, experiences, and behaviors is often the only thing that helps to resolve them. Therapy can be a very supportive experience. The psychologist, social worker, or family therapist providing the treatment is trained to help the child and family feel safe. He or she knows that it can be difficult to seek therapy and wants to make sure that the family gets help in a respectful and reassuring way. Sometimes it just feels very good to have someone who listens and understands, and who has ideas about what might help to make things better.

Families can also find help without therapy. Family meetings allow time for every member of the family to talk about his or her experience and to ask for help with problems. It is important to pick a time that the whole family can be there. Then, unplug the phone and turn off the television so everyone can focus his or her attention on the meeting. People need to talk one at a time. Sometimes it helps to have an object to hold that signifies whose turn it is to talk. This can be anything: a hat, a coaster, a stick, a piece of cloth. The object can be passed

Many different kinds of therapy are available. Teens can often get counseling right in their schools. (Guidance counselors and teachers can provide information about services offered at school.) Therapy groups are also available, and schools often know how to find them. Pediatricians will also have recommendations for good therapists. Usually the therapist will want to know the history of the problem and some information about the teen and the family. The therapist may do some teaching about things that might help, or may focus on trying to help the family uncover its own solutions. A family has the right to change therapists if the match does not feel like a good one.

around, but only the person holding it may speak. It is important to be sure that everyone has a turn.

Time-out can also be helpful when families are having trouble. Sometimes during a fight or argument, people are simply too angry to work on resolving the problem. It can help to agree to take ten to twenty minutes to settle down, and then to address the problem more quietly when everyone is calm. Adults as well as kids need to practice time-outs. Time-out is not the same as punishment. It is simply a decision to table the discussion until people can speak calmly and respectfully.

Middle schoolers and teenagers also get a great deal of support from their friends. It is important to spend time with friends and to talk with them about what is happening at home. Friends are particularly important for people in this age group. Remember that withdrawing from friends and social activities is a warning sign. Support from peers can be essential when things are stressful. (Teens also still need to spend time at home and to have these conversations with their families.)

There are also books and associations that provide extra support, information, and resources to stepfamilies.

A Reminder About Normal Families

Stepfamilies are normal families. They can feel wonderful, and they can also go through hard times. Understanding stepfamily issues may help teens remember what is typical and what is a warning sign. There are millions of stepfamilies in this country. Being a part of one is a common event, and can be a very happy part of life.

Chapter Notes

Chapter 1. What Is a Stepfamily?

1. Interview with Zach (not his real name), June 1998.

2. P. C. Glick, From "The 1987 National Survey of Families and Households" presented at Address to Annual Conference, Stepfamily Association of America, Lincoln, Nebraska, 1991.

3. J. Larson, "Understanding Stepfamilies," *American Demographics,* vol. 14, 1992, p. 360.

4. L. L. Bumpass, R. K. Raley, and J. A. Sweet, "The Changing Character of Stepfamilies: Implications of Cohabitation and Nonmarital Childbearing," *Demography,* vol. 32, 1995, pp. 425–437.

5. J. A. Sweet, L. L. Bumpass, and V. Call, "The Design and Context of the National Survey of Families and Households," National Stepfamily Association for Demography and Ecology, 1989.

6. Mala Burt, ed., *Stepfamilies Stepping Ahead* (Baltimore: The Stepfamily Association of America, 1989), p. 2.

Chapter 2. How a Stepfamily Is Formed

1. Interview with Zach, June 1998.

2. Interview with Sam (not his real name), May 2000.

3. Interview with Mary (not her real name), August 2000.

4. American Academy of Child and Adolescent Psychiatry, "Stepfamily Problems," 1997, <http:www.aacap.org/web/aacap/publications/factsfam/stepfmly/htm> (April 29, 2000).

Chapter 3. Living in Two Houses

1. Interview with Emily (not her real name), May 2000.

2. Interview with Zach, April 2000.

3. Interview with Sam, May 2000.

4. Interview with Jason (not his real name), April 2000.

5. Interview with Leslie (not her real name), May 2000.

6. Interview with Hannah (not her real name), March 2000.

7. Interview with Sam.

8. Interview with Zach.

Chapter 4. Stepparents as Parents

1. Bobbie Reed, *Merging Families: A Step-by-Step Guide for Blended Families* (St. Louis, Mo.: Concordia Publishing House, 1992), pp. 9, 56.

2. Interview with Ted (not his real name), May 2000.

3. Interview with Hannah, March 2000.

4. Interview with Zach, June 1998.

5. Interview with Hannah.

6. Ibid.

7. Ann Getzoff and Carolyn McClenahan, *Stepkids: A Survival Guide for Teenagers in Stepfamilies* (New York: Walker and Company, 1985), p. 33.

8. Ibid.

Chapter 5. Parents as Partners

1. Interview with Sam, May 2000.

2. Interview with Jason, April 2000.

3. Interview with Leslie, May 2000.

4. Interview with Sam.

5. Interview with Zach, June 1998.

6. Interview with Sam.

7. John Gottman, *The Marriage Clinic: A Scientifically-Based Marital Therapy* (New York: Norton and Company, 1999), p. 35

8. Interview with Hannah, March 2000.

9. James Bray and John Kelly, *Stepfamilies* (New York: Broadway Books, 1998), p. 24.

10. M. Fine and L.A. Kurdeck, "Relation Between Marital Quality and Stepparent-Stepchild Relationship Quality for Parents and Stepparents in Stepfamilies," *Journal of Family Psychology*, vol. 9, 1995, pp. 216–224.

Chapter 6. Gay Stepfamilies

1. Interview with Jason, April 2000.

2. Ibid.

3. Janet M. Wright, *Lesbian Stepfamilies: An Ethnography of Love* (New York: Haworth Press, Inc., 1998), pp. 69–95, 145–192.

Chapter 7. How Does It Feel to Be in a Stepfamily?

1. Interview with Ted, May 2000.
2. Interview with Jason, April 2000.
3. Interview with Emily, May 2000.
4. Interview with Hannah, March 2000.
5. Interview with Leslie, May 2000.
6. Interview with Zach, June 1998.

Glossary

divorce—The legal ending of a marriage.

family meeting—A time set aside for a family to talk about their experiences together without interruptions.

half-siblings—The brothers and sisters who are the children of one of the original parents and a stepparent.

original family—The family into which the child was first born or adopted.

siblings—Brothers and sisters.

stepfamily—A family made up of an adult couple, at least one of whom has children from a previous relationship.

stepsiblings—The children of a parent's new partner.

therapist—A professional who is trained to help individuals and families understand and resolve important life experiences.

Internet Addresses

The Stepfamily Association of America
    <http://www.saafamilies.org>

Stepfamily Foundation
    <http://www.stepfamily.org>

The Stepfamily Network
    <http://www.stepfamily.net>

Parents Place
    <http://www.parentsplace.com>

Further Reading

Aydt, Rachel. *Why Me?: A Teen Guide to Divorce and Your Feelings.* New York: The Rosen Publishing Group, 2000.

Coleman, William L. *Step Trouble: A Survival Guide for Teens with Step Parents.* Center City, Minn.: Hazelden Information & Educational Services, 1993.

Ford, Melanie, Annie Ford, and Steven Ford. *My Parents Are Divorced, Too: A Book for Kids by Kids.* Washington, D.C.: American Psychological Association, 1997.

Isler, Claudia. *Caught in the Middle: A Teen Guide to Custody.* New York: The Rosen Publishing Group, 2000.

Leibowitz, Julie. *Finding Your Place: A Teen Guide to Life in a Blended Family.* New York: The Rosen Publishing Group, 2000.

Marshall, Peter. *Cinderella Revisited: How to Survive Your Stepfamily Without a Fairy Godmother.* North Vancouver, B.C.: Whitecap Books, 1996.

Sanders, Pete, and Steve Myers. *Stepfamilies.* Brookfield, Conn.: Millbrook Press, Inc., 1995.

Smith, Gloria V. *From Trials to Triumph: The Portrait of a Family.* East Elmhurst, N.Y.: Manchester Publishers, 1998.

Stern, Ellen S., Evan Stern, and Zoe Stern. *Divorce is Not the End of the World: Zoe's & Evan's Coping Guide for Kids.* Berkeley, Calif.: Tricycle Press, 1997.

Index